"As one who has worked with thousands of single moms across the country, I find this book to be fascinating. Not only did I find myself pregnant 4 times by the time I was 19, but I had NO guidance in this area. Connie Firmin puts words around a dialogue that any young woman (or those who work with them) can use and implement into their every day lives. With 17 million single moms in this country, sexual purity is a hot-button topic and *Sparkle* is the answer!"

\- Jennifer Maggio, author of *Overwhelmed*
and *The Church and the Single Mom*

"As a mom of three girls, I understand how intimidating it can be to begin a conversation with them about purity. I am so glad Connie Firmin has given us moms such a fantastic (and Bible-based) tool as a launching pad! Not just for my girls to read, but also for me and my husband to read, too. *Sparkle* is a must-have tool for every parent to have in their library."

\- Molly Venzke, Seattle WA

"*Sparkle* is such an encouraging book with practical wisdom for girls facing the challenges of exercising purity in today's world. Connie speaks with spiritual maturity that comes only from learning lessons the hard way and then growing in the Lord. As a result God has used her because of her own experience."

—Brenda Messina, Baton Rouge, LA

"As a youth pastor for over 8 years, I have witnessed first-hand the fight it takes for us girls to keep our sparkle. The pressure we feel from movies, magazines, music, tv, our girlfriends and guys to be sexy is always there. I've talked to numerous girls who feel nothing but regret after giving away their purity to that guy or girl who they thought they'd be with forever, only to find out that forever only lasted a while. So what do we do when the pressure to fit into our sexual world gets to be too much? What do we do when we've dulled our sparkle and given away our purity? Is it too late?

Sparkle is a book every preteen, teen, woman, mom, daughter, friend and chick should get a hold of and never put down. Whether your a girly-girl, tom-boy or somewhere in the middle, this book will meet you right where you are and help you to chip away at the smudge that you've got hiding your divine sparkle and teach you how to maintain your luster. I highly recommend it, and wish that every girl would sparkle just as God intended you to do so! There's nothing more stunning than a girl who sparkles in purity. The world is watching…"

—Crystal Tullos, Youth Pastor at Healing Place Church (2002–2010), Baton Rouge, LA

SPARKLE

SPARKLE

Reflecting Purity in Today's World

CONNIE S. FIRMIN

TATE PUBLISHING & *Enterprises*

Published by Tate Publishing & Enterprises, LLC
127 E. Trade Center Terrace | Mustang, Oklahoma 73064 USA
1.888.361.9473 | www.tatepublishing.com

Tate Publishing is committed to excellence in the publishing industry. The company reflects the philosophy established by the founders, based on Psalm 68:11,
"The Lord gave the word and great was the company of those who published it."

Book design copyright © 2011 by Tate Publishing, LLC. All rights reserved.
Cover design by Amber Gulilat
Interior design by Nathan Harmony

Published in the United States of America

ISBN: 978-1-61777-565-9
1. Religion / Christian Life / Relationships
2. Family & Relationships / Peer Pressure
11.05.05

DEDICATION

To Miley and Kamryn:

May each of you seek to live lives of purity and run after God with everything in your sweet little hearts.

ACKNOWLEDGMENTS

To Renee' and Micki:

You girls probably know most of this book by heart. I know some of my greatest speeches were given to both of you. Thanks for being such a shining inspiration to me each in your own unique ways. May you sparkle like the diamonds God created you to be. I love you both!

To Doug:

Thanks for listening to me talk about this dream for *many* years and helping me to take it from vision to reality. I couldn't have done this without your love and support. Thank you for always standing by me and putting up with all the girls' connect groups, sleepovers, Amplifieds, and every other thing I've volunteered our home and help for. You are the best, and I love you!

To every person who helped along the way:

(and you know who you are!)

Your input, ideas, prayers, and, most of all, encouragement have been priceless for me. Thanks for believing in me, reading manuscripts, listening, praying, editing, inspiring, and being a part of my dream. You are as much a part of this book as I am, and I am truly grateful for each one of you. I wish I could list each and every one of you by name, but there just isn't enough space.

Most of all, to God:

Wow, what a journey it's been. I owe You the highest credit! May Your words leap off the pages of this book into the hearts of every reader. Without You, these words would simply be empty rambling. You have healed me from the inside out and taught me Your view of purity along this awesome adventure. May true purity spread like wildfire.

TABLE OF CONTENTS

FOREWORD

Sometimes, as a pastor, I've had the chance to see people really step into a place of serving and leading and being part of the vision of the church in a way that demonstrates the awesomeness of God's ability to guide and direct our lives. Connie Firmin and her husband, Doug, are two of those people. DeLynn and I are so thankful for the blessing that it is to have Doug and Connie at Healing Place Church. Their heart to serve and their passion to help others grow in their relationship with Jesus is a true representation of the heart of this church and of the heart of God, too.

One of the greatest challenges in our world today is purity—particularly in young people's lives. There is an incredible amount of promiscuity thrown in our faces every day through media and advertising, as well as just how many people dress and speak.

Many times when I was a youth leader, I would hear messages and read books that offered help in this area, but their answer was to simply isolate and avoid traps. This book isn't just about avoiding what's wrong, though.

Connie does a great job of giving proactive ways young people can move forward in relationship with Jesus, and in doing so, they'll find a new strength to keep themselves pure sexually and in every way.

It's not enough just to try really hard. And it's not enough to really just want to be pure and to try to avoid seeing and hearing things you just don't want in your mind. All of that is important, for sure. It's just not going to be enough. What it takes is an avid, growing, and thriving relationship with Jesus Christ. I have seen so many times a young man or young lady make a commitment to purity in their life and what always seems to make the difference is their relationship with Jesus. The closer you get to Jesus and the more you pursue Him and His love and plan for your life, the more you experience the power of purity. And purity is an incredibly powerful force.

DeLynn and I want to encourage you to read this book with an open determination to do whatever it takes to get yourself where God wants you and to do life His way. In doing that, you'll experience more life and more purpose and destiny than you ever imagined possible. And you'll find yourself right in the place where God can use your life to help others find the opportunity to experience Jesus and His saving grace.

—Dino Rizzo
Lead Pastor
Healing Place Church
dinorizzo.com

INTRODUCTION

I am so honored to have the opportunity to share my heart with you. My quest began a few years ago when I started studying God's passion for purity and answered His call to write my story. He's taken me on a journey through my own life to an amazing place of healing, and I only share a snapshot with you on these pages. My prayer is that you will avoid some of the potholes I hit in the road of life.

As a teenager, I remember looking at myself in the mirror and wondering, *Who is that girl?* I did not recognize the person in the reflection, nor did I feel I had time to worry about it then. I was too busy planning out my future. *Am I going to attend college? If so, what do I study? When will I see my boyfriend again?* You know...the important things of life! I was busy trying to be the person I thought everyone else wanted me to be. I found myself empty and aching. I desperately wanted to be freed from the person I had become. Somewhere along this road, I managed to take a detour from the real me. I just wanted to be the authentic person I was on the inside ... to be me! Only I didn't know how I would get there.

Then the unthinkable happened. While in twelfth grade, I found myself pregnant, confused, and scared. How in the world would I get through this situation? Could I fix it? Decisions I made created this alternate route, causing a great deal of pain in my life. I had to put my plans on hold because I was going to have a child of my own now. My life changed in an instant, and God used the situation to change my heart. Through the years, He has taken my heartache, restored me, and showed me that I am of royal heritage ... a daughter of the King! He's given me a purpose and a destiny.

Speaking of royalty, I'm sure there are lots of records (probably many books) on the proper behavior of the members of the family. I imagine the children born into the family study this beginning at a young age until they have memorized every detail. Every person in the royal lineup has a role and duty that they are expected to carry out with class and flare according to a set code so that they will bring honor to the royal name. God has prepared the same for every person—man or woman, young or old! He has a duty for each of us. He blesses us with gifts and talents to make this destiny reality, and as stated in Psalm 139, He's written our days in His book before even one came to pass. The Bible should be our focus— our road map, if you will—and we should study it our entire lives.

As you read this book, you will see *Check It* sections. These will help you expand on the information contained in the chapter and relate it to your own life. In this section, I will give you some things to journal about and an occasional assignment. Journaling is a great way to express your thoughts and discover new things about yourself. You'll also discover *Store It* Bible verses throughout the entire book for you to commit to memory. I strongly suggest learning these verses by heart. Yes, I know…you have enough things to remember for school, but I promise this is easy and well worth the time. The Bible is our instruction manual for life. Just check out 2 Timothy 3:16–17. I believe in studying God's Word; I consider it crucial to understanding purity in today's world. You may even see random *Ask It* questions to think about throughout chapters and some occasional quotes.

Finally, I am only a simple human being obedient to God's passion inside of me to spread this simple message. I strongly suggest that you research what you read on these pages. Talk it out with others you respect, pray about it, see if it lines up to God's Word, and then pray some more. Please do not take one word of this book as truth without checking into it for yourself. My purpose in writing this book is to help you understand God's view of purity and empower you to live the life that God intends for you to live. I hope the stories I share from my own life speak into yours.

May God reveal His message through these pages to you so that you will grow closer to Him and seek Him and His guidance for your life…a lifestyle of purity!

THE SPARKLE

As I sat in the divided classroom, I had one thought in mind: How the heck do I get out of this? *I had a teacher who loved to do activities with the class. She especially enjoyed having classroom discussions on the things no one else wanted to discuss. We tackled tough topics like alcohol, drugs, and drinking and driving…you know, the big guns. Today's topic: For or against sex before marriage? Our activity would spark quite a bit of discussion and controversy among the students. The instructions were simple. "If you believe it's okay to have sex before marriage, step to the left side of the classroom. If you believe in waiting to have sex after you are married, go to the right." Not bad. I'd just walk over to the right, blend in where no one would notice me, and then head back to my seat. For once, despite my previous and current lifestyle, I would take a stand for something I personally had begun learning the hard way. To my amazement, I was nearly alone with only few others as the majority of the entire classroom stepped to the left. What was I thinking?*

Then the teacher took it a step further, asking us to defend our stand. Talk about being singled out. No blending in unnoticed here. The students on the other side of the classroom became furious with us as we tried to defend ourselves. I recall stating, "Having sex before marriage, especially as a teen, leaves you with feelings you are not ready to handle, and the consequences are deep." You see, I was experiencing this lesson firsthand. I thought I had handled my answer with bravery and wisdom. To my dismay, the other side of the room erupted into comments like, "Who are you to tell me what to do? I'm eighteen and that makes me an adult, old enough to make my own choices…" and "We all know the consequences…babies and diseases! Heard that one a hundred times! Blah, blah, blah!" The one that hurt the most was "What do you know? You're not even a virgin!"

The last comment was stinging my heart to its core as the teacher regained control of the class. Who did they think they were to attack me? I knew what I was doing was wrong, and I didn't like where it had led me. I knew the truth! The sad part was, although I wanted out, I could not fix the problem on my own. I did not know where to begin or how to help myself. I felt so empty on the inside and powerless.

Purity…I wanted it! What happened to my vow of waiting for Mr. Right? How did I get into this relationship leaving me powerless and empty on the inside? All of the not-so-great decisions I previously made were almost too heavy to carry anymore. Somewhere along the road of life, I had taken a detour. Deep down inside, I wanted to get my life back on track, but I just didn't know how to get there. My classmates obviously disagreed with my idea, my teacher just listened as we all argued, and my boyfriend…well, he certainly would not approve of the new change. What was this girl to do?

Purity: What Does It Really Mean?

We must first realize purity is more than a casual choice. I believe it's a way of life. I like to think of it as the sparkle inside of me. You might ask, "What is purity anyway?" Most of us think purity is simply not having sex before marriage, which is partly true…but it's so much more than that.

Check out some of the definitions for purity that I found on the Web[1]:

- The condition or quality of being pure; freedom from anything that contaminates, pollutes, etc.

- Freedom from guilt or evil; innocence.

- Physical chastity; virginity. *(Note: Chastity is a really old word for abstinence or having no sexual relations)*

Did you notice what two of these definitions had in common? The word *freedom*. Purity is a lifestyle of freedom. In order to be pure, you have to be *free* of contaminates and pollution. Think about it this way: Diamonds…they are a "girls best friend," right? When you go to the jeweler, you wouldn't pick a diamond that's cloudy-looking or flawed. No, you'd go for one that sparkles the most. You'd look at things like cut and clarity, as well as color and carat weight (size of the diamond). The one with great clarity and color would allow its true beauty to shine through. If the diamond is cut properly, then light can properly reflect through the top and make it come to life, which is what we all love to see…the sparkle. Make the wrong cuts on the diamond, and the flaws distort the diamond's real beauty. It's the same with your picture of purity.

I am a visual person, so I relate to things I can picture in my mind or actually see. Freedom is basically the opposite of slavery. When I think of slavery, I imagine people working hard, possibly chained up, unable to make choices for themselves, or at the mercy of another person. I picture freedom as a butterfly floating where it may in the air, unbound by anything, guided only by the wind. Freedom is like that. It has no restraint. If we are chained to our past experiences or tied to our impurity, we are like the slave. We are held captive, meaning we are unable to move about freely without hesitation. If a slave were suddenly freed after years of captivity, he or she would most likely not know how to make decisions for him or herself. After years or a lifetime of bondage and powerless to make free choices, their bodies may be free to go where they wish, but their minds would be frozen with fear, probably scared to make any decisions. God wants us to be free like the butterfly guided by the wind so we can follow His guiding hand where He leads.

Upon leaving the classroom that day, I felt powerless because I was chained to the past decisions I had made, presently frozen in fear, and unsure of how to make healthy decisions for my future. I was a slave. I had no clue what the Bible had to say about purity. In fact, I had not even read an entire chapter of the Bible at that point in my life. I believe the reason we tend to struggle in the area of purity is that we have not learned what God's Word says about it. God has me on His mind constantly through my own royal legacy (my life). The same holds true for you. God requires obedience and faith from all of us—obedience in daily living to follow His desires, and faith to believe that He has our best interests in mind. If we don't know what the truth is, then we are powerless to live it out, which leads me to the next crucial point in order to fully understand purity: There is a difference between God's view of purity and the world's view.

Godly Purity in Today's World

Sex is everywhere. Just look around. We are surrounded by the world's version of purity. Almost every place you go (online or in person) or whatever channel you select on the TV, this counterfeit edition is in your face. Sometimes it's difficult to tell the difference. Here are a couple of things to consider when deciding if it's God's version or the world's version:

The world says purity can be whatever you decide.

The world has taken *pure* right out of *purity*. It has tried its best to separate purity from God and dilute (water down) its meaning into just another word. There are countless phony versions of purity, leaving so many people confused, stranded, and downright injured.

God says purity is a way of life that saturates every part of who you are.

I want you to grasp that purity is worship to Jesus. It isn't just another word. It affects how you think, what environments you choose to be a part of, and what you speak. It changes your perspective on everything and allows you to see clearly. Look at the lives of those around you that God has transformed. Look at the stories of the great men and women in the Bible whose lives were radically changed. Stories like Ruth, Rahab, David, Paul, Moses, Esther, Mary, the woman caught in adultery, and the list goes on—countless accounts of transformed hearts. They all have the same story of God's great love reaching into their lives and making them pure and beautiful. Be pure God's way!

Ask It: What if everyone defined purity as God does?

The world says sex is just what you do to fit in or be considered normal.

According to the world, you should try out sexuality before you get married so that you can make sure you find just the right person. They say everyone's doing it. What do they think they are shopping for? Shoes? I don't know about you, but none of that sounds right to me. Besides, when you are shopping, you eventually have to decide on a pair of shoes in the end. All that shopping makes me tired and leaves me confused and empty.

God says you don't need to fit in to be normal. God's version of purity is more than just refraining from sex. It is His way of protecting you from diseases, a bad reputation, and, even worse, slavery (remember purity is about freedom). God created purity in the beginning and never intended for it to change. Evidently, in the early days, someone thought they would *improve* what God started, and it's been a mess ever since. Purity is all about guarding your heart and being holy before God. It doesn't mean you are perfect. The world says it's okay to experience pleasure at any cost, but God calls us to have self-control (Galatians 5:23 (NLT)).

Ask It: What if the world embraced purity to be cool and normal? Would it make our decision to be pure for God any less difficult?

Sparks Fly

I'll tell you a little secret of mine: *I love jewelry!* Unfortunately, my budget just cannot afford my taste. You know, there's something about the sparkle of a diamond that catches the attention of every girl's eye. When held in the light, it puts on a show like no other. Just like a diamond, we must be pure on the inside to reflect the light from within us to the world around us.

Throughout the coming chapters, I want to present purity from a new perspective. I believe it's all about perspective. You and I can view purity as something that holds us back, or we can view purity as the ignition in our lives. I believe we were all made to sparkle like diamonds, catching the attention of those around us. My question is this: What are you reflecting? What sparks fly from your life into the lives of those around you?

We're about to take a journey through God's Word to see some of what He has to say about this topic. I don't want you to miss one thing, so buckle up! It's going to be a wild ride. I hope you're along for the adventure.

Check It:

In the *Check It* sections, you will be given questions to think about and/or journal about. It is my hope that you'll really think about how this book relates to your own life. Remember, there are no right or wrong answers! It's a journey, not just meaningless busy work. I can't wait to see where we end up together.

- Either below or in your journal, take some time to write about what you would like to learn about purity. What would you like to learn as you read through these pages and about your relationship with God?

Store It:

> For God has not given us a spirit of fear and timidity, but of power, love, and self-discipline.
>
> 2 Timothy 1:7 NLT

People are like stained-glass windows. They sparkle and shine when the sun is out, but when the darkness sets in, their true beauty is revealed only if there is a light from within.

—Elizabeth Kubler Ross

BENEFITS OF SEX BEFORE MARRIAGE... NOT

*"We'll call you this afternoon when we get the results."
This was the only comment the nurse made as she left the
room. It was 9:00 a.m., and there would be approximately
seven hours before the phone would ring with the news. I
drove to the house where I waited for the call. Oh, the pressure! This, by far, was the biggest mess I had gotten myself
into yet. I tried to keep my mind off the phone that wasn't
ringing. A million thoughts ran through my head. What
would I do about school? Would he marry me? What
would my parents say? What would my friends think?*

*With my future in its grip, the phone rang. I took a
deep breath and answered the call. "Hello?" The person
on the other end of the line was about to give me information that would change my life from that day forward. I
hung on every word she spoke. "The test came back positive. Congratulations! You'll need to get with the appoint-
ment desk to schedule your next visit." It seemed as if I*

was in the middle of a nightmare I just couldn't wake up from. I was eighteen, unmarried, and pregnant.

My boyfriend and I both sat in the living room in disbelief. Was this just a dream? Did she really just say I was pregnant? Somehow I usually managed to get myself out of everything I got into, but not this time. What were we going to tell everyone? Would I be expelled from school? I only had a few more months until my high school graduation. What about my college plans? How would we pay for this? Would we get married? With so many questions racing through my mind, all I could do was lie down on the couch and cry.

Christmas is my favorite holiday of the year! I love giving (and getting) gifts. The girls in my family have some great traditions, such as making Christmas candy together to give as Christmas gifts (a story within itself), and my all-time favorite: family shopping on Black Friday. The day after Thanksgiving, Black Friday, is supposed to be the biggest shopping day of the year for Christmas gifts and ultimate sales. It's definitely the craziest day! My sister, my daughters, and I get up at the crack of dawn year after year to wait in long lines and see some of the funniest sights. Our mission is to find the perfect gift at a great price, but I think one of my favorite parts is watching the people.

Thinking of shopping gave me this view. Imagine this scenario with me for a moment: Your mom has completed all of her shopping. She's bought all of your Christmas gifts, but you have no idea what she has purchased for you. You wake up early one Saturday morning to find that you are the only one awake. As you quietly enter the living room, you spot the Christmas tree glowing with all of your beautifully wrapped gifts just sitting there. No gift should ever be left alone, right? All of the suspense is getting to you. Since your parents aren't around, you think, *It won't hurt to take one tiny peak.* So you carefully unwrap one side of the first gift only and take a little glimpse. You see something that sparks your interest, but you can't quite make it out. Gently, you peel back the tape from the other side. You see more of the gift but not enough to fully know what it is. Quickly, your guilt begins to get the best of you so you tape the paper back as it was before and decide to wait for the surprise. Besides, your little brother could come barreling down the hall any minute, and he blabs on you for everything! The coast is clear, and no one will ever know you peaked at the gift.

You spend the entire day consumed with thought about your gift. Trying to figure out what you saw, your imagination runs wild. It's all you think about. You find yourself waiting for everyone to go to sleep that night because the curiosity is killing you! You plan to take one more quick look. No one will know. As soon as everyone's asleep, you run to the tree where the presents are waiting for you. You unwrap it slowly, but with increasing speed, until suddenly you realize your mom got you a new iPhone since the dog ate yours earlier this year! You are so excited that you decide to remove the tape from the next one, and the next one, until finally you've opened all of your gifts. You cannot believe all of the great gifts your parents bought you, but all of a sudden, instead of being able to enjoy them, you are full of regret that you didn't wait a couple more days to be surprised Christmas morning.

Sex is just like that. You start small, but the curiosity kills you. You become more interested with what's beyond just holding hands, and then kissing, and so on. You find yourself "unwrapping" your gifts meant for your future spouse. You unwrap one and then the next and the next. You may decide, "What does one little kiss hurt anyway?" It's not that it hurts anything, but it puts you in decision mode. From there, you begin making decisions about when and where you will draw the line. Decisions like *Should we make out? Where will I let him touch me?* and *How far is too far?* have to be made. Honestly, if you are asking "How far is too far?" the real question you want to know the answer to is "How close to sin can I get without actually sinning?" That is one dangerous loaded question. At the end of the road, most people decide that it was a mistake to unwrap any of those gifts before the right time. Why not wait until "Christmas morning," when the excitement is at its highest point, to open your gift where you can do so without the guilt and shame? You'll enjoy the experience much more if you wait.

Sex is not a bad thing until it's taken out of the boundaries of marriage. There is nothing shameful about sex in marriage. When you meet Mr. Right, you will be attracted to him. God created you this way, but He wants you to save the gift of sex for your spouse. While you are waiting, He is building character within you. God desires you to love yourself the way He loves you before you experience this gift. Sex is a beautiful expression of love between a man and woman that are married to one another, and it isn't intended for any other atmosphere. God's standard is hard and often misunderstood in the twenty-first century; however, there is honor in waiting. You can make purity a priority.

Great Things about Being a Virgin

Many young people feel there are plenty of benefits of having sex before marriage and feel being a virgin is a disgrace, but God's Word says it is beautiful and an honor. I want to rearrange your thinking by giving you five reasons to strive to be a virgin. We will start with number five and work our way back, David Letterman style, to the best thing about being a virgin until your wedding night.

5. You will have a great reputation

Has anyone ever told you, "Your reputation precedes you"? It's true. Sometimes we think no one will find out what we do, but the truth is that the world loves a great story. In fact, the juicier the story is, the better. Magazines are filled with story after story about people who live wildly. You know you've read them! Personal stories about who is dating now, which couple got divorced, or who was recently arrested. I think you get the idea.

This point brings to mind the summer before eighth grade. At that time in my life, I was certainly not living for Jesus nor listening to what God wanted for me. I thought a guy was the solution to the emptiness I felt inside. So after telling my mom a lie about where my friend and I were going, we went to a party. Since I wanted to be cool and they were drinking alcohol, I began drinking too—an unwise decision. I nearly became the victim of rape that night. Had my mother not come looking for me when she did, I would have been taken advantage of in one of the worst ways possible. More about that later.

As you can imagine, this was indeed a juicy story. I was teased unmercifully by the guys who were at the party after that night. The girls in my neighborhood wanted nothing to do with me anymore. As the story spread by my so-called "friends," my reputation was extremely smeared. The tale became twisted from what really occurred, and the rumors were out of control. I am sure you know it is vicious out there. I doubt you need anyone to tell you this, but you do need to know the truth. Your reputation speaks volumes about who you are long before you even enter the room. A great reputation conveys to others that you are strong, confident, and secure in who you are without ever having to say a word about yourself. You simply shimmer to everyone around.

4. You won't get pregnant.

I don't think I need to go into a lot of detail in this area. It is no secret that you must have sex in order to get pregnant (unless your name is Mary and you are over 2,000 years old). Just to clear up any confusion you might have, let me state that having a baby will *not* fix any of your problems. Alarming statistics show that the pregnancy rate for US teens has decreased since the 1990s, but the stats are still high. I did some searching online and found over 445,000 babies were born in the United States in 2007 to teen girls alone ages fifteen through nineteen. [2]

Sometimes when we hear numbers like that, we just tune them out because it's hard to imagine. So let me paint the picture for you. At our local university, Louisiana State University, the Tiger Football Stadium has 92,400 seats. If you were to fill up every seat with a teenage mom holding her newborn baby, you would fill nearly five stadiums for each teen mom to have a seat in this one year alone (not to mention that this is counting only United States teen girls and only the ones actually giving birth). Whoa! I don't know about you, but this number is alarming to me. It's a lot of teen girls and a lot of screaming babies. I think it should be our mission to reduce that number drastically.

You can do this by making the decision to remain a virgin before marriage. A great guideline is to never be alone or in private with a guy for any reason. The places and situations you allow yourself to be in with a date should be chosen carefully. Watch your body language and what you say to guys. Also, be careful about what you listen to from guys. Some guys will sugarcoat empty promises with statements that sound great at first. God wants His girls to be pure, to be virgins, to be radiant. Most of all, He wants His girls to love Him and know that He loves them! Hang on, chicks! He will give you the strength you need to wait.

3. You will not get STDs.

There's a good bit of information about the different types of sexually transmitted diseases (STDs) out there. However, most of the websites (not just church sites) I researched agreed that the best way to avoid getting an STD is to abstain from sex altogether. Even the world agrees on this fact: Abstinence is the best policy for avoiding STDs.

Today's youth are challenged with so many things. Friends with benefits, oral sex, homosexuality—and this list could go on for days. No wonder we're so confused! Unfortunately, it seems that teens think oral sex is the new "safe sex." It is not safe at all. In case you didn't know, you can get STDs from oral sex. Unfortunately,

STDs from oral sex are rapidly spreading among teens. It is our job to become educated on consequences of pre-marital sex so that we can reduce the risk.

2. You'll be able to tell your groom on your wedding day, "I saved myself for you."

Being a virgin enables you to say with full confidence your past is one of purity. Carrying baggage from your past into your marriage is destructive to your intimacy, and you will not want your future husband carrying any baggage from his past into the relationship either. When you find the man of your dreams, you will want to give him your whole heart—an undamaged heart. Sex is a gift from God that produces life and closeness between a married man and woman. God doesn't say that you should use that gift for anything else. God desires you to be pure for Him. What do you expect of your future husband? Shouldn't you hold the same value for yourself?

Proverbs 31:10–12 (NLT) says, *"Who can find a virtuous and capable wife? She is more precious than rubies. Her husband can trust her, and she will greatly enrich his life. She brings him good, not harm, all the days of her life."* You are alive now, right? That means you are a gift for him now. Not just from the day of your wedding on, but the Bible says *all* her life. That means since the day you were born. Don't open your husband's gift. It will spoil the surprise.

Drum roll, please! And the greatest reason for being a virgin until your wedding day is...

1. You are living the life God intended for you to live.

Living God's way is by far the best thing you can ever do! God has a plan for your life that far exceeds anything you can ever hope for, dream up, or imagine for your life. If you are living in God's will, you allow yourself to hear from Him. When you're sexually active before marriage, you entangle yourself in a web of guilt that will bind you spiritually and eventually cause you to be unable to move. That's one reason why being sexually active goes against God's intent for your life. He wants you to be free so that He can use you for His purpose.

Let's sum up everything in three words: *Wait for God!* He alone will direct your path. Every girl is just one bad boyfriend or one unhealthy date away from making choices that will impact her future. Make sure you don't fall into that trap. Your future husband is out there, and he's trying to grow up in this crazy world too. Girls, you've got to take a stand. Make it your priority to lower the numbers of teens with STDs, the number of teen girls filling up that stadium, and the number of teen girls filling up on guys instead of God.

Restore Me

Now some of you may be thinking, *I've already made choices to be in a sexual relationship.* You may feel valueless or dirty from your past decisions, or you may think you have no choice now and cannot turn back. The truth is that God wants to restore you, regardless of where you've been. *God loves to scrub out the spots in our lives and make us whiter than snow.*

The world loves to plant thoughts of how we ruined ourselves and how unforgivable we are into our minds to distort our beliefs. John 8 describes the woman Jesus defended who was caught in adultery. I imagine the world must have tried to fill her mind with so many lies as she stood there guilty and helpless. However, Jesus taught this woman with love. Jesus challenged the men from the community to throw their stone first if, and only if, they were without sin themselves. The men left dropping their stones one by one. After the last guy left, Jesus asked her who was there to condemn her. Her reply was, *"No one."* He lovingly told her in John 8:11 (MSG), *"Neither do I. Go on your way. From now on, don't sin."* Jesus wants us to embrace the same love He generously gave the woman in this verse and to turn from our sin as He instructed her to do.

Here are some steps to help begin your journey of restoration:

- The most important step will likely be the hardest. You must make the decision to change. Others will likely not understand your choice and may even give you some flack about it. Let them. Do not listen to anyone who says you cannot walk away from being sexually active and start fresh. Once you make the decision, walk away and pray about it. Ask God to forgive your sins, to give you strength to avoid those situations, and to restore your purity.

- Secondly, find a leader or friend that will support your decision to change. This should be a trustworthy person who will pray for you—someone there when you need encouragement to stand strong and can give you not only good but godly advice. Get involved in a good local church if you are not already in one. You have to get connected and have a support system in place.

- Next, I would suggest walking away from the relationship. It will be extremely difficult to stay in relationship with a guy without continuing the sexual part. Seek to be in relationship with Jesus before getting back into any relationship with this guy or any other. Remember, only Jesus can fill the vacant place in your heart. Any other relationship or object we attempt to fill our hearts with will only leave us empty.

If you will step out in faith, God will definitely meet you on this journey. He will take your past and create the most beautiful masterpiece of wholeness in your life! Let me assure you, He is an expert in this area.

Check It:

- How can you help to lower the alarming teen statistics (teen pregnancy, STDs, etc.)?

- Are your actions supporting or opposing this cause?

- Is there anyone that you know struggling in this area? Don't write their name down, but pray for them. Maybe share with them some of the things you learned so far, or let them read your copy of this book when you are finished with it, or give them their own copy to read with you.

Store It:

Create in me a clean heart, O God. Renew a loyal spirit within me.

Psalm 51:10 (NLT)

From the abundance of the heart the mouth speaks. If your heart is full of love, you will speak of love.

—Mother Theresa

WHAT GOD'S WORD SAYS ABOUT PURITY

*I had read all of the horoscopes, and so far, none had
come true. Not even when I tried to make them happen.
I had taken all of the boyfriend quizzes and love tests I
could find in* Seventeen *magazine, but this particular
quiz promised to have all the answers I was looking for.
I had one question: Do I have sex to keep a relationship? It seemed that was the answer, according to my
friends and what I watched on TV, but I wasn't com-
fortable or certain.*

*I turned to page 81, grabbed a pen, and curled up
on my bed. I answered every question carefully, totaled
my score, and read the results.* "Ready, set … wait! You
might not be ready yet. Waiting doesn't mean forever." *That was it?! That was the answer?*

*The truth was what I wanted, but I was left confused.
Why would the quiz say,* "No, wait," *when my friends
and everything around me says,* "Go for it!"*? I needed
answers. Could someone help?*

As a young teen, I recall seeing the latest versions of all of my favorite magazines at the register every week when we grocery shopped. It was as if they were calling out to me, waiting for me to buy a copy to bring home. Sometimes I would try to grab one and toss it in the buggy, hoping my mom wouldn't notice. When we'd get in the car, I would dig it out of the bag and quickly flip through the pages, soaking up all the advice I could get. These magazines seemed to have all the answers to life's most important questions. There were articles on everything from hair and makeup to dating and flirting. The only problem was I still wasn't finding answers to my deepest questions. How would I ever know if no one told me?

God's Word speaks about purity in many ways. I love that His Words are written for us like our very own "Owner's Manual" to life. We have so much to learn from the Bible. As I have studied about purity, I've learned God has a lot to say. Sometimes you have to dig to find answers, and other times it falls right off the pages into your lap.

So What Does God's Word Say about Purity?

There are several references for purity. For starters, let's take a few pointers from 1 Corinthians 6:18–19 (NLT):

> Run from sexual sin! No other sin so clearly affects the body as this one does. For sexual immorality is a sin against your own body. Don't you realize that your body is the temple of the Holy Spirit, who lives in you and was given to you by God? You do not belong to yourself.

In this verse, I see some key points I want you to notice. First, God strongly expresses His feelings about sexual sin. He doesn't say you can flirt with it. He doesn't announce to us to just glance the other way or try not to think about it. Nor does He state to casually walk away from it. He says *"Ahhhh! Run away! Run for your life!"* Would you stand still in the yard if bees were chasing you? No, I don't think so. You know you'd run like a wild woman with your hair caught on fire. God wants you to do just that. He doesn't want you to just avoid sin; He wants you to run away from it as if your life depended on it (and honestly, it does).

Secondly, this verse tells us that we should be pure because the Holy Spirit lives inside of us. If you have accepted Christ as your Savior, then you are a treasure chest that holds and protects the treasure of the Holy Spirit. Yes, that's right! You can have the actual Holy Spirit living inside of you. Not only do we learn that the Holy Spirit lives inside of us, but it also says to glorify God *in* your body, not outside. God is concerned with what goes into our bodies. When you guard your body, you are in essence guarding your purity.

The verse continues on in 1 Corinthians 6:20 (NLT), saying, *"For God bought you with a high price. So you must honor God with your body."* Newsflash: *You do not own your body.* As mentioned above, you are a treasure chest holding the riches of the Holy Spirit inside your heart. Treat your body as if it really is God's. You don't have the right to abuse or misuse your body or anyone else's, for that matter! Take care of your body and love it the way God made it. It is of great value to Him, and He has entrusted you with its care. Fortunately for us, Jesus died on the cross for the sins we each committed, and His death paid our bill in full. This bill we each owed was something that we could not pay for on our own (together or alone), and He just wiped it away. Since Jesus paid our full debt, we should honor Him with our bodies by setting ourselves apart from the crowd. When we value and love our bodies enough to protect them, then we are worshiping God with our purity.

The Sky's the Limit

God also mentions some things He does want for you. I believe we'll need some of these things to pursue purity and reflect it to those around us. The Bible describes these as "fruit." Galatians 5:22–23 (NLT) states:

> But the Holy Spirit produces this kind of fruit in our lives: love, joy, peace, patience, kindness, goodness, faithfulness, gentleness, and self-control. There is no law against these things.

You'll definitely need things like patience and self-control. The best part is there is no limit! You can have as much of this as you want! Notice how God calls them the *fruit* of the Spirit, which is singular. This means that God doesn't want you to have just a few of them. He gives you the green light to load up on all of them as if they were one item. As you pursue purity, you'll ultimately develop this kind of fruit. Note: You cannot get this fruit by works. Everyone has some type of fruit in their life. Living a life of careless choices and away from God will produce fruit, but it will be stinky, rotten fruit. Aspire to have good fruit, just like mentioned in 1 Timothy 4:12 (NLT). It reads:

> Don't let anyone think less of you because you are young. Be an example to all believers in what you say, in the way you live, in your love, your faith, and your purity.

I love the part that says to "show yourself an example of those who believe." You should be sparkling in the area of purity so that people around you will see purity through your words and your actions. People are always looking to the examples of others. I think Jesus's life was probably the greatest model of purity in the Bible. He is a glistening illustration of purity for our own lives (1 John 3:3, MSG). Remember, purity isn't an opportunity; it's a way of life.

Serving with young people for several years, I've listened to stories of regret and tales of what seemed like relationship nightmares. One thing most of these chicks had in common was they had lost their sparkle somewhere along the way. They believed the lie the world offered them and didn't know the truth. They all wanted the answers, but they didn't want to take the time to find them or just didn't know how to search for them. They settled for the cloudy and polluted versions of life the world presented them.

Psalm 119:9 (NLT) gives us a glimpse into the answer: *"How can a young person stay pure? By obeying your word."* Living a life of purity can be clear-cut if you follow God's direction. We need to get into the Word. It can actually be an amazing adventure as you experience all that He has planned for your life.

> …he added: "Take to heart all the words of warning I have given you today. Pass them on as a command

to your children so they will obey every word of
these instructions. These instructions are not empty
words—they are your life!"

Deuteronomy 32:46–47a (NLT)

In this verse, Moses reminds the people to make their
lives revolve around God's Word. Make your life revolve
around God's Word and watch purity begin to shimmer.
When God's Word is priority in your life, God is able to
take you on an amazing adventure. Moses tried to instill
God's value into the people he was leading, but they
rejected his teaching. The result was wandering around
in a desert for forty years! Whoa! What a long time. We
should not only study God's Word to see what His desire
is for us in the area of purity but in every other area of our
lives as well. I don't know about you, but I don't want to
wander for forty years in a desert.

Recap

Let's sum up the meaning of purity. Purity is freedom
from anyone or anything that would cause sin in our
lives. The process of purity is:

1. Protect the Holy Spirit that lives inside of us by guard-
    ing our hearts and bodies.

2. Value the price that was paid for our freedom by hon-
    oring God with our bodies and producing good fruit.

3. The answer to staying pure is found in God's Word. We need to make it a priority in our lives.

In summary, don't let the world's empty and irresponsible view of purity define you. Watch the cycle unfold in your life. As you make God's Word a priority in your life, you will run from sin. When you run from sin, you are protecting the Holy Spirit that lives inside of you. When you protect the Holy Spirit, you are worshiping Jesus and valuing the price that He paid for your freedom. Now that's what I call sparkling!

Check It:

- Do you consider yourself *sparkling*? Why or why not?

- Challenge: Make a list of questions you have about purity. Start digging around in God's Word for answers. Make sure you list the verses you find.

- Idea: Get a spiral-bound set of note cards. Write down all of the verses you find about purity and read them often.

Store It:

God blesses those whose hearts are pure, for they will see God.

Matthew 5:8 (NLT)

You're blessed when you get your inside world—your mind and heart—put right. Then you can see God in the outside world.

Matthew 5:8 (MSG)

Purity of mind and idleness are incompatible.

—Gandhi

THE INVISIBLE BACKPACK

Finally, I decided I had discovered this man of my dreams. He fit all of the conditions I had: tall, blond, attractive, muscular, tan, and mature. Although I thought I was pretty mature and would catch his attention, what I really needed was a plan. I had to meet this guy. He was having a party one night, and my good friend's brother was going to be there. Perfect! We'd just tag along with my friend's brother. The plan was coming together nicely. I'd meet him, and the rest would be history. So I lied to my mom about where I would be, put the hottest outfit I could find into my bag, and off I went.

Once we were there, the group decided to spice up the party with a little alcohol. Since I had not yet caught the prince's attention after thirty minutes, I thought I'd be cool by drinking, even though I was only thirteen. Besides, I needed to be swept away by 9:30 p.m. and it was already 8:00 p.m. What I had not planned for was quickly becoming drunk, and I soon passed out. I recall only bits and pieces of the night, thankfully. The moments I do remember are almost too much to handle. I never caught that guy's eye, but unfortunately, I did grab his cousin's attention.

My friend eventually left me at the party because I was drunk, and after regaining some consciousness, I found myself in a dark bedroom, half dressed, and about to be raped. I so desperately wanted help! Since I was not home on time, my mom frantically began searching for me. Once she located the party, she busted through that bedroom door like a warrior, and just in time, she rescued me. She became my knight in shining armor that night.

Have you ever tried to be someone you're not? The summer before eighth grade, oh, I tried, all right! I began to dream of being whisked away by a knight in shining armor. I romanticized how he would be able to fix all the wrongs in my life; he would unconditionally love me for who I really was inside. He would never lie to me. We would live together happily forever. I tried to be someone else to hide the real person I was inside.

Each one of us has a backpack we carry everywhere we go. No one can see our backpack because it is invisible. No one knows what we place inside of it. Many times we fill it with invisible masks that we think hide the parts of our lives we do not want others to see or, worse, makes us someone we are not. A mask is anything we can hide ourselves behind. At the party, I tried to wear several different masks, which got me into serious trouble. Sometimes we pick up a mask based on the opinion of another person or from past experiences we had in life so we can hide a wound. Sometimes we grab one after watching a TV program because the show made us think about ourselves in an unpleasing way, and other times, we just like the mask. Any way you look at it, it's hiding the *genuine* person God intended for our lives.

Can I be real for a minute? At times, I have struggled with being a "people pleaser." Pleasers (as I like to call them for short) are basically people who want to please other people. In other words, they want to gain their acceptance or approval by doing or saying what they think the other person may want to hear or see. They struggle with being who they really are because they feel it may not be good enough to the other person. I believe we become pleasers when we don't make the decision to be who God created us to be and we put on masks. One of the best choices we can make is the decision to see ourselves as Jesus sees us. Thankfully, He doesn't see you and me the way we see ourselves at times. He sees us as beautiful, valuable, and precious.

I began loading my invisible backpack many years before the night of the party. At the young age of seven, my grandma told me a huge family secret. This was massive and changed my life the instant I heard it. As I had done so many times before, I spent the night at my grandma's place, only this time, she woke up early to tell me what she knew. You see, I had no idea my biological father died when I was around nine months old. My mom had remarried when I was two years old and she, along with my new dad, decided the right time to tell me about my father's death would be when I was older. My new dad adopted me as his own child when I was young, so I had no clue. My dad was my world, and I loved him like no other. My grandma felt the secret could wait no more, and her news crushed me. *Who could I trust now?* I didn't know what to believe anymore.

Trusting no one, and I mean *no one*, I decided I would never allow anything or anyone to hurt me like that again. At the time, I didn't understand my parents, in their own way, were in fact trying to keep me from pain, while my grandmother simply felt the secret was dishonoring my biological father's memory. This big family mishap created deep wounds in my heart. I picked up that invisible backpack, and I loaded as many masks into it as possible. I hid every part of who I was and began creating the "me" I wanted to allow others to know. Any hint of a sparkle in me was covered up, buried alive. I carried my invisible backpack every place I went. I thought by hiding the real me, I wouldn't be hurt like this again, when in reality, I only created a "pleaser" attitude, longing for the approval of others.

After the near-disaster at the party where I was to meet my knight in shining armor, I loaded even more masks in the invisible backpack. The backpack had become heavy and hard for me to carry. I thought everyone knew my dirty little secret. My "so-called" friends teased me and made me feel worthless. I felt like I had a huge red X on my forehead that everyone could see. I wanted to be the popular girl everyone looked up to and adored, but instead, I became the girl no one wanted to hang around. I constantly worried about what people thought about me. I did not know how to act around others because I hid behind so many masks. I was surrounded by a wall of doubt and confusion about who God created me to be. Since I didn't read my Bible and did not have any accountability in my life, I tried to wear the identities of other people as my own. I didn't know who the true "me" was. Now that I am older and free, the most comical part is I don't want to be like the people I considered to be so wonderful then. I wonder what made them so attractive to me in the first place. I believe the key is I had no standards for my life.

You may not have the same story, but you do have the same decision to make. It is simple. Don't get me wrong; your outer appearance is important to God, but He wants you to shine on the inside as well. When you start to see the *amazing beauty* that God personally placed within you, you will naturally begin to see your beauty on the outside. Your beauty is waiting to be unveiled! God used His bare hands and created you so that you will accomplish wonderful things for Him. He has a purpose and a destiny for your life that no one else on this earth can accomplish like you can.

> *Ask It: What are you going to live for? Are you building your self-worth on your looks, on what others think about you, or on the potential Christ created inside of you? Will you see yourself through God's eyes or the world's glasses?*

The decision is yours. Choose to live a life full of adventure and promise based on who God created you to be. Purity will fall into place if you have this part down. Remember, purity is not just sexual; it's a lifestyle. Part of being pure is deciding not to believe the empty promises of others based on their mere words. You will not be as tempted to speak, act, or dress the same because you will value yourself as a daughter of the Most High, a royal princess sparkling for all to see.

Check It:

- Do you seek to please people or to sparkle for God?

- What's in your *invisible backpack*? Do you need to clean it out?

- Did you discover anything about yourself from reading this chapter?

Store It:

Guard your heart above all else, for it determines the course of your life.

Proverbs 4:23 (NLT)

In order to succeed, your desire for success should be greater than your fear of failure.

—Bill Cosby

FILL 'ER UP, PLEASE

What was taking so long? I could hardly stand it. My dad and my uncle went to check out a car, possibly to buy for me, and they had been gone for what seemed like hours. After many discussions, my dad and I decided to find an old Mustang to restore. It probably wasn't the dream car of most girls my age, but it was mine. We talked about paint colors, interior stuff, and a new radio. Every night I had pictured (and driven) the finished product in my dreams, and it was a-ma-zing!

When they finally pulled in the driveway, I saw the car. Amazing wasn't quite what came to mind. Oh, what a mess. It certainly wasn't what I had pictured. I wondered how that was going to be transformed into something beautiful. I'd have to see the transformation to believe it. How could anything good ever come of this heap of junk?

Until now, we have been talking about purity in some pretty broad terms. We've talked about diamonds and sparkling to others through your life. We have discovered purity is much more than just sexual purity. It's about a lifestyle of purity—what I call "the sparkle from inside."

Now I am about to shift gears, spending the remainder of the chapters talking about purity in regards to relationships. You might think, *Oh no! Here she goes talking about my boyfriend!* Au contraire! In this chapter, we will talk about your relationship with God.

Believe it or not, your relationship with God will determine the outcome of your dating life. Yes, you read that correctly. If you are completely or partially disconnected from God, you will likely have a great deal of heartache with relationships. Therefore, it is important that you get really connected to God *before* you begin the process of locating the true love your heart's been dreaming about: Mr. Right.

At fourteen, I was constantly dreaming about the day when I would begin driving. I couldn't wait! I thought freedom would be all mine. The funniest part of the entire fantasy was I had no realistic view of what driving would be like.

When you begin driving, you quickly learn it costs a lot of money. An entire book could be written on this concept alone. Initially, the expense of the vehicle is generally the largest amount required. Then there's the cost of learning to drive in driver's education classes. Oh, and don't forget about insurance. It's required on the driver and on the vehicle that you get to drive. If that isn't enough, regular maintenance must be performed on the vehicle to keep it in good running condition. And no matter how well you take care of your car, there's always an accident or breakdown that can happen, costing you major bucks for repair work to fix the damage! Last, but certainly not least, there is the big one: the cost of the fuel. Unless your parents are willing to shell out the big bucks to pay for everything, you will have to spend some of your free time working to earn money for the awesome privilege of driving.

You are built much like a vehicle. Maintenance (sleep and exercise) and fuel (food) are required to keep your body fit and running. They cost time and money as well. Planning ahead is a necessity in this department. Sadly, when you have the desire to eat, there isn't an award-winning chef standing in your doorway, ready to make the meal of your choice at no cost to you. Don't get me wrong here; it would be awesome to have a personal chef, but it is not reality for most people.

The Heart of the Matter

When thinking of the word *heart*, one might picture a muscle pumping blood to various parts of our bodies or maybe the red thing we draw all over our love notes—both of which are correct. Did you know that you have a spiritual heart as well? God created your spiritual heart to be filled by Him and Him alone.

Your spiritual heart needs maintenance and fuel just like your body or vehicle. Without these items, it will become hard, calloused, and unsatisfied, unable to pour out or receive as God designed it to function. Just like a vehicle, it *will* cost you something to fill it up. I want to unpack three requirements for your spiritual heart:

Requirement 1—Time: Every single thing you do costs you time. Surfing the Internet, eating, texting, talking on the phone, doing homework, watching TV, sleeping—whatever it is, time is at stake!

Requirement 2—Fuel: You need fuel for each thing you do. As I mentioned before, over the life of your driving career, fuel is probably the most underestimated cost of driving. If your car's gas tank is almost empty, you will have to stop to fill it up or your car simply will not run much longer. No exceptions! Unfortunately, cars will not run on Oreos and ice cream (yet).

As I mentioned earlier, you require fuel just like a vehicle calls for gasoline. Eating no food or unhealthy food does not fuel your body properly. If you eat junk food all of the time and do not exercise, your body will lose resistance to illness and disease, and you will not feel your best. For your spiritual heart, junk food is not a choice either. You must have healthy food. You may think this is just a repeat of what I said about the car, but it is not. Let me explain.

If you fill up your heart with junk and do not feed your relationship with Christ, you will starve. When your heart is starved, it will crave to be filled with something. Hungry hearts can be *extremely* dangerous! If you are not careful, you can fill it with counterfeit fuel, leaving you empty and broken down. Many girls attempt to ignore the hunger pains of emptiness by using TV, food, texting/phone calls, friends, boyfriends, and more to temporarily fill the emptiness and attempt to forget about the hunger pains. At first, masking the sting is easy. But before long, the little things that hid the hunger no longer cover the pain. The search for something larger to fill the emptiness and hide the damage starts back up again. Eventually, even the large objects no longer fill the empty spot. I have a revelation for anyone reading this: *A relationship with Jesus is the only true fuel that will fill up your heart!* It was created specifically for this purpose.

Hang that on your mirror and/or in your locker at school. Memorize it. When you feel yourself gravitating toward bogus fuel, say it over and over again. It is the truth! Jesus is the only fuel that will not leave trash or buildup in your gas tank. God placed a reservoir in each of us that is intended only to be filled by Him. Just like when you drive your car, there is no better feeling than when you have a full tank of gas. Make sure your heart tank is filled up!

Requirement 3—Maintenance: Like cars, you and I need maintenance. Your relationship with God and fueling up your spiritual heart are activated by munching on the Word of God. Educating yourself in the Word will save a lot of heartache that will eventually require heart repair. God gave us an "owner's manual" just like a manufacturer puts an owner's manual in every new car. When a light comes on in your dashboard or something breaks on your vehicle, you will either read the owner's manual for your vehicle or consult a mechanic. Our owner's manual is called the Bible, and our mechanic is Jesus. God's Word instructs us in so many areas. It teaches us, gives us guidelines to live within, and encourages us in our future. To be honest, Jesus knows how to fix everything with one tool: His blood.

If you are still saying, "This maintenance stuff is new to me! What do I do now?" then here are some suggestions for you:

1. First you need to dedicate some time for God each day. Some refer to this as *quiet time* (QT for short). This should be uninterrupted time (if possible), so turn off your TV, cell phone, and/or computer. Your friends will be fine for a short while—I promise. You can call them later to tell them about your QT. It helps to start your

day off by focusing on Him before you do anything else, but you can have QT anytime, anywhere. I would set aside fifteen minutes to begin. There's no set format. Play worship music, sing to Jesus, pray out loud, journal about what you read in the Bible, or simply read your Bible. Change it up from day to day. Before you know it, you'll be spending much longer than fifteen minutes.

2. Get a good devotional book. There are so many types out there: topical books, daily books, age-specific books, gender-specific—just pick the one that is the best fit for you.

3. Pick a scripture each week and memorize it. Yes, I did say *memorize* it. Try to pick a verse that applies to something you are dealing with in your own life so that you can use it. In Joshua 1:8 (NLT), God's Word says that we should meditate on the scripture day and night. The people mulled over them, which means they repeated it, studied it, let it sink deeply into their hearts. Make it the verse you choose to study for the week. Pick it apart. It is amazing what God will teach you in this process.

With the proper time, fuel, and maintenance, you'll have your spiritual heart purring like a kitten. Let me restate from the beginning of the chapter that your relationship with God will determine the outcome of your dating life and all of your other relationships. Make sure it's the best it can be!

Check It:

- Are you spending your time well?

- What kind of fuel are you using in your spiritual heart's tank? Does it need a change?

- When is the last time you did any maintenance? Are you overdue?

- Don't forget to make that sign for your locker or mirror: *Jesus is the only true fuel that will fill up my heart!* Make it personal ... add your name.

Store It:

Whom have I in heaven but you? I desire you more than anything on earth.

Psalm 73:25 (NLT)

To keep a lamp burning, we have to keep putting oil in it.

—Mother Teresa

BEAUTIFUL FROM THE INSIDE OUT

As I stared at the return address on the envelope, I wondered how they came across my name. Miss Teen Louisiana? Several weeks before, I received a letter with an invitation to apply for their upcoming pageant. I thought, Why not? I wasn't afraid to try anything. In fact, I pretty much had tried it all, from sports to gymnastics to music. I filled out the application, wrote a letter saying all the things I thought the panel would like to hear, and mailed it off with some recent photos. Dreams of one day walking down the runway and being handed beautiful roses as someone placed a tiara on my head floated through my mind. Would I even have a shot at winning the title? Like most other young girls, I wanted to be seen as beautiful.

The long-awaited reply to the application was now in my hand. Gently, I opened the envelope, carefully pulling out the response. As I unfolded the letter, I couldn't believe my eyes. I was in! I had been selected to actually participate. Was it a mistake? Was I dreaming? I wondered what they saw in me. Could I live up to all I was on paper? Would I trip on the stage or, worse, make a complete fool of myself? My excitement quickly turned to fear. After all, it was a "beauty" pageant.

As we discussed in the last chapter, understanding and accepting God's love makes you pure, but loving yourself and studying God's Word is what keeps you pure. You might be saying, "I understand the studying God's Word part, but what about loving myself? How do I do that?" Well, we are going to tackle that now.

"Real beauty is in the eye of the beholder!" Have you ever heard this quote before? I have to admit, I don't know who said that, but I'm pretty sure that their eye didn't have to look at all the stuff we have to look at! Today in America, beauty is all too often defined by a person's outward appearance only. It's seen all through movies, music, the malls, magazines, MTV, and the Web. We are led to believe that our beauty depends on our hairstyles, makeup, weight, clothing—and the list goes on. It's almost as if our entire lives are a pageant.

On a recent trip, I noticed how breathtakingly creative God is. In the first chapter of the book of Genesis, we read how God created the world, and as I flew over many countries and bodies of water, I personally saw some of His incredible creation. As I experienced different landscapes, each completely beautiful and unique in its own way, I realized that God doesn't like things to look the same. He loves variety! There are flat lands, oceans, deserts, mountains, lakes, ice lands, waterfalls, rain forests, and so much more. Some regions are hot, some are cold, and some are just right. Some even sparkle. I could go on for days. I began to think that if the earth is this beautiful, what must it be like in heaven? I cannot wait to see it!

Psalm 139 (MSG) says God sculpted each of us, and as He made us, He again expressed His creativity and beauty. He not only made the earth unique and beautiful, but He planned us to be rare and lovely also. He placed a combination of traits no one else can recreate inside and outside of each individual person. If God intentionally designed each of us to be completely different, then why do we try to act like, talk like, dress like, and look like every other person we think is beautiful? Our real beauty is just waiting to be revealed, but we must discover it, tap into it, and then display it. In order to discover and display your real beauty, you must first love yourself. This is the beginning of your breakthrough.

I Love Me, I Love Me Not...

When I was a teen, if I could get someone to notice my clothing instead of my body, I felt better. I tried hiding behind my clothing as if it was a disguise—yet another mask from the invisible backpack I carried around. Instead of trying to camouflage ourselves, we need to learn to love our bodies they way they are. God loves us just the way He made us. Would you get a paintbrush out in front of Picasso and adjust his painting? Would you rewrite the lyrics of a song in front of your favorite band, saying that their words just don't fit? Not likely! Why should we tell God what a "poor" job we feel He did when He created us?

When I was fifteen, my new hair stylist, JoAnn, took me under her wing and showed me a thing or two about hair and makeup. Once I learned how to tame my frizzy hair and apply makeup according to my coloring and facial features, I began to like the girl I saw in the mirror. I was like the ugly duckling that turned into a beautiful swan. Suddenly, guys that had not given me the time of day began to talk to me, and I let it go straight to my head. Confidence in the person I was on the outside began to grow. I liked this new girl I saw in the mirror; however, I still didn't know who was on the inside. My new looks didn't make me any happier, although it did get me noticed. I based my identity on what I physically saw in the mirror, but I didn't change what I looked like on the inside. I quickly started digging in my invisible backpack for masks again. I felt so trapped and wondered what was wrong with me.

I'm Supposed to Look Like That?

Why do we feel like we need to change our appearance? I think it's because we compare ourselves to people who are not authentic, and we allow others to set unrealistic standards for our appearances. Before the pageant, I spent countless hours scanning through TV programs, watching every movie to see what I could do to improve myself. I read every magazine I could talk my mom into buying. I took every quiz to see how I ranked. Even with all of that information out there, I did not feel better about the girl I saw in the mirror. I was confused. I wanted the truth! I was trying to mesh all of these ideas together into a person who would be acceptable to those around me rather than being acceptable to God. No one was interested in the fake version of me. What they really needed was for me to be confident in the girl I was created to be.

Today's "on-screen chick" has had many hours of hair care, workouts, makeup, and, in some cases, surgeries. Many times her photos have been edited to take out any imperfections. Many of the women we call beautiful are not what you see in person. We see what Hollywood feels to be acceptable instead of an average female. Airbrushing is used to increase or reduce weight, enhance curves or features, and more.

How can we possibly compete with an airbrushed body in a photo? The truth is, we can't! If we attempt to judge our own bodies by that standard, we will almost always fail. No woman has a flawless body. If you asked any one of those girls in the pageant arena to point out something she did not like about herself physically, regardless of how outwardly beautiful she may be to you and me, the majority—if not all—of them would immediately point something out. We are all like that. Many of the few perfect-looking women on the big screen have had surgery or procedures to make their bodies more pleasing to the eye.

A dear friend of mine struggled with an eating disorder. She thought she needed to be smaller until she finally hit rock bottom. She had to seek professional help in order to overcome the "ideal" she had dreamed up as normal. Guess where she got this image from? Yep, that's right! She got those ideals from TV, movies, and magazines. If you find yourself wanting to look like that Barbie you see on TV, then take a break from TV. Are you watching the same movie repeatedly and dwelling on the fact that you don't look like the actress with the perfect body? Give it a break. Don't watch it.

The truth is, we are not put on this earth to soak up worldly ideals but to revolutionize the world! How will we do that if we are trying to blend into the world? If we could just get this into our minds, life would be so much simpler. Through my teens and into my twenties, I was unable to see who I really was, even though my eyes were wide open. When I finally made the choice to see things from God's view, I saw how empty my lack of faith left me. I had to learn to see myself through God's eyes and find out what He loves about me. If you focus on your positive qualities and love yourself the way God loves you, you won't need anything else to define you.

But I Don't Love Myself

Okay, so if staying pure requires loving yourself, then you are going to need a few pointers on how to do just that. I realize in this world today, it's really hard not to get caught up in the comparative game. With that in mind, I have a secret mission for you to accomplish in the *Check It* section. I hope you will choose to accept this assignment, but beware; it just might change your view. You might begin developing shimmering self-love.

You will need to get a pen and your journal for this task. Please set aside some time to complete this. You won't get much out of it if you rush through it in three minutes flat. Before you read further, make a decision to complete what is written here and pray about it. Remember: it is a choice.

Check It:

Stop here: Ask God to open your eyes to His view of you. Pray for His beauty to become real and personal to you before you go any further.

Mission: "Improve the View"

Make a list of the positive qualities about yourself. This list could include qualities about your appearance, your character, your achievements, or anything that makes you feel good about yourself. Some of you may be thinking that you don't have anything to list, but if you think hard enough, you can come up with at least a few things. I have listed some examples below for you:

Smile	Eye color	My love for God
Polite	Dedicated	Loyal to friends
Smart	Hair (only on non-humid days)	Heart to serve others

I know it's hard, but the point is to see the great qualities of ourselves. Sure, we can take the time to make a huge list of the things we don't like, but how will that really help us? Try to have no less than ten items on your list. Note: You can list as many as you would like. In fact, the more the better! Do not go to Step 2 until you complete Step 1.

Take your positive list and separate it into inward qualities and outward qualities. Compare your two lists. If your list is mostly outward qualities, try to add some inward items. If mostly inward things are listed, come up with some things you like about your outward appearance.

Note: You are going to keep this list. You should review it often and continue adding things to it.

Ask another female that you look up to (your mom, older sister, teacher, youth pastor/leader at church, etc.) to make a list of only the good *qualities they see in you.* Chances are their list may be larger than your own. Ask them to be honest and positive. Compare this with the list you created; you may want to add some of these to your list. It's cool to see your positive qualities through another person's eyes. Sometimes we learn great things about ourselves this way.

Make a list of only *two things that you are unhappy with that you* can *change. Then write one or two simple steps by each one that you can do to make a difference in this area of your life.* Make a choice to work on one or more of these qualities that you see needing improvement.

Here's an example:

Problem area:
When someone insults me, I immediately lash out at them.

Possible solutions:
Try counting to ten in my mind before responding so that I will not say things I will regret later.

Memorize Psalm 4:4 (NLT) and recite it when I feel like lashing out.

Once you master these areas, make a new list and work on them. Soon, your positive list will be growing, as well as your love for yourself.

Store It:

How precious are your thoughts about me, O God.
They cannot be numbered!

Psalm 139:17 (NLT)

You are what you are and you are where you are because of what has gone into your mind. You change what you are and you change where you are by changing what goes into your mind.

—Zig Ziglar

THE PURITY DECEPTION

Love was in the air that night, and I was looking in all the wrong places. My family was attending a wedding reception for a close family friend whose younger brother was like my own brother. Several of his friends were there, so the prospects seemed promising.

As I walked over to get a bite of wedding cake, I heard my name from across the room. I couldn't believe it, but my friend was actually going to introduce me to one of his friends. I had been waiting for this day! As he walked over with this dark-haired dream, my heart skipped a beat. How should I act? Cool? Not interested? Interested? The only problem was I was actually desperate for some form of love. I'd take anyone willing to show me attention.

My friend introduced me to John, and I was hooked. His dark, curly hair and dark eyes were so inviting. We danced a little and talked a lot. I felt a lot like Cinderella, hoping the clock wouldn't strike 12:00 a.m., and when it did, I didn't want to leave. What I didn't know was my friend and his buddies thought it would be funny to introduce me to John.

They thought I wouldn't be interested and he'd be shot down by me. It was all a joke from the beginning.

Have you ever looked at something only to realize it wasn't what you thought it was? I sure have. Looking back at the night I met "John" (not his real name), I should have known something wasn't right. Since I had allowed my definition of love to be tainted, I didn't see anything coming. I was blinded.

Why is the world so worried about the Bible's version of purity and love? Honestly, I don't really understand it myself, but it's happened. The world has been distorting the love Jesus displayed for us during His life for centuries—distorting everything that reminds us of Jesus. It mocks all of what God has created, especially in the areas of love and sex. Men and women have struggled with temptation since the time of Adam and Eve. The serpent tricked Eve into taking just one bite of that fruit, and that is the same trick the world uses on people today. If we can be lured to take one bite, then the devil can and will use that one bite to ruin our view of love and sabotage the call from God on our lives.

God desires us to have pure love. He wants us to practice love that is not selfish, love with no strings attached. It is the same love Jesus displayed to us when He walked with the disciples and the people of His day. In John 15:9 (NLT), Jesus says, *"I have loved you even as the Father has loved me. Remain in my love."* Other versions say that He calls us to *abide* in His love. *Abide* means to await, to submit, to remain in, or where to reside. He calls us to await His love, to submit to His love, or to reside or live in His love. Doesn't that sound like such a safe place to be? It gives me a warm, fuzzy feeling. Had I pursued love like this, I would likely have avoided many of the heartaches I experienced in my teens and twenties. The devil hates this kind of love, which is known as *agape* love—love that is unconditional and has no boundaries. God has given us His version of love in 1 Corinthians 13:4–7 (NLT). I am sure you've seen or heard it before. It's on Valentine's cards and is sometimes read at weddings.

> Love is patient and kind. Love is not jealous or boastful or proud or rude. It does not demand its own way. It is not irritable, and it keeps no record of being wronged. It does not rejoice about injustice but rejoices whenever the truth wins out. Love never gives up, never loses faith, is always hopeful, and endures through every circumstance.

I especially love The Message version of this verse:

> Love never gives up. Love cares more for others than for self. Love doesn't want what it doesn't have. Love doesn't strut, doesn't have a swelled head, doesn't force itself on others, isn't always "me first," doesn't fly off the handle, doesn't keep score of the sins of others, doesn't revel when others grovel, takes pleasure in the flowering of truth, puts up with anything, trusts God always, always looks for the best, never looks back, but keeps going to the end.

The world's version of love is completely opposite and might look like this:

> My love is impatient; why should I wait? My love is unkind and jealous; I can brag and act arrogant and unbecomingly if I want to! My love seeks its own,

why should anyone come before me? I am easily provoked and offended, I keep score of *all* wrongs, and my love doesn't forget anything. Why should I forget? It approves of unrighteousness and lies; my love hates the truth. My love puts up with nothing and doesn't believe anything. It's all hopeless anyway! My love endures nothing and *always* fails.

I encourage you to stop here and read the true version of 1 Corinthians 13:4–7 (NLT or MSG) again. Take five to ten minutes to allow God to direct your heart. Meditate on what it is saying. Break down each line. Write down anything you see in your life that doesn't line up with God's type of love or if you see anything that lines up with the world's version. Pray and ask God to fill you with His love. Ask Him to help you change those areas in your life so that you will have His true love and not a worldly view of love.

The world tries to substitute sex in the place of authentic love. If you try to swap the word *love* with the word *sex* in the NLT or MSG versions above, it doesn't fit. The truth is that sex and love cannot be defined the same, although the world tries to convince you otherwise. True love will wait for God's timing. The world wants you to believe that jealousy is an appropriate response in a relationship when it actually just destroys the life within it. True love will not be full of green-eyed envy or suspicion. In the world's version of love, it is boastful, self-centered, bragging at all times, and is not considerate of another's feelings. We know God's love is not boastful or self-seeking. It is about building up people around you by being positive and lifting those around you to a higher place through encouragement, support, and love. It seeks to give God glory and doesn't seek its own glory. The fake version of love offered by the world always fails, but God's love is forever!

As we mentioned before, purity is not just about keeping boundaries in the area of sex but in all areas of your life. That is by far one of the world's biggest schemes. According to the world, sex is wrapped into the picture with anything and everything. The world seems to be fixed on that area of life. It seems to be the quickest and easiest target for attack. God desires our motives in every decision to be pure. He wants us to love our neighbor as ourselves. He wants us to be pure in conversations, as well as in our thoughts and actions. Beyond that, He wants us to love our enemies. To be successful, we have to be pure in our motives.

Ladies, this might hurt a little, but if we are gossiping, envious, insecure (this list could go on for pages), is that really what loving our neighbor is about? Pure love doesn't spread rumors. It is not vicious. Wishing your classmate's boyfriend would just dump her or that her hair would frizz is not pure love. Girls can be horribly mean to one another. It is time for this generation of women to take a stand. It is time to change the definition for girls everywhere. We need to radiate purity in every part of our lives. We need to sparkle with God's love. In the words of one girl: "Purity is about being the best you can be in everything."

Check It:

Look over your notes from 1 Corinthians 13:4–7 in the exercise above, and then make a sign for your bathroom mirror with this verse. Read it every morning to remind yourself of God's love.

- Write a song or poem to Jesus about true love in your journal.
- Tell Him how much you love Him and thank Him for His love.

Store It:

Love is patient and kind. Love is not jealous or boastful or proud or rude. It does not demand its own way. It is not irritable, and it keeps no record of being wronged.

1 Corinthians 13:4–5 (NLT)

God is not only the answer to a thousand needs; He is the answer to a thousand wants. He is the fulfillment of our chief desire in all of life. For whether or not we've ever recognized it, what we desire is unfailing love. Oh, God, awake our soul to see—you are what we want, not just what we need.

—Beth Moore

TO DATE OR NOT TO DATE—THAT IS THE QUESTION

When I got home from school, I couldn't wait to talk with John. I thought about him all day, talked to my friends about him every possible minute and rushed home to wait for his call. We had been dating for nine months now. When the phone finally rang, my heart leaped inside. It's him!

Me: Hello?

John: Hey, you have a minute? We need to talk.

Me: Sure, what's up?

John: I don't want to hurt your feelings, but I'm about to be a senior, and I'm just not sure anymore. I need a little space.

Shocked, I hung up the phone. I began to sob. What did I do wrong? I thought everything was great. I gave him everything I had to give. What was I supposed to do now? My heart hurt so much. I didn't want to talk with anyone, so I cried myself to sleep.

At fourteen, I was ready to find the guy of my dreams. I thought to myself, *This will be the one thing that makes me happy about who I am!* Sound familiar? My parents allowed me to begin dating a guy that was seventeen. Life was grand! John was older and more mature than I was. We attended different high schools and lived on opposite sides of the town. Not only did he drive, but he also had his own vehicle. At the time, I felt this relationship made my so-called "friends" more accepting of me. Actually, it only made me more aware of how I didn't measure up to their standards. The infatuation consumed me! It affected my grades, my morals, and my identity.

Then it happened. After nine months of dating, John broke things off. How could this have happened? I had been a good girlfriend, right? I did all the right things I read in the magazines and saw on the talk shows. I was always available when he called and made time for him to go on dates around his schedule. Heck, I had recently started having sex with him when I really wasn't prepared to have that kind of relationship yet. My friends told me to get over John. How could I? He was everything to me, or so I thought.

A week after the big breakup while I was still moping around, my friend Jaye came by to visit. He was like a brother to me and knew my ex-boyfriend. He had to hear the same sad story from me about being dumped and how I would wait for John. I was a "faithful girlfriend," even if it was only an ex-girlfriend now. My friend encouraged me and told me I deserved better. He decided what I really needed was to go to the movies and get out the house. He said some fresh air would do me good. What I didn't know was Jaye knew who else would be attending the movie that night.

As we walked into the movie theater, we recognized some of our friends from school and headed straight over to them. It was like a movie scene. The entire group immediately parted like the Red Sea with every eye on me. Standing directly in front of me was John. I stood there frozen and speechless in what felt like hours staring at what I saw. He was on a date with another girl and holding her hand, just days after breaking up with me. It sure didn't take him long to recover. Actually, he had broken up with me for another chick. I was heartbroken! Instead of allowing me to be blinded by the world's version of relationship, Jaye brought me face-to-face with reality. It hurt like crazy, but I am so thankful for the truth. He said I was worth so much more than I believed.

The decision to date can be a tricky decision. The bad choice I made to date John had nothing to do with my boyfriend but had everything to do with my focus not being on the right target. So what is the right target? The Bible is packed with endless principles about dating and love. 1 Corinthians 7:34 says (NLT):

> In the same way, a woman who is no longer married or has never been married can be more devoted to the Lord and holy in body and in spirit. But a married woman has to think about her earthly responsibilities and how to please her husband.

I believe this verse is filled with tips regarding dating. Let's break it down.

This verse tells us that the young person choosing not to date can easily focus her sight on God. There is no one else to please daily. No distractions. Drama is not separating her from sitting at Jesus's feet or following His will for her life. She has time to hear from God when she is not with her friends. She is not seeking anyone else's approval or affection—just God's acceptance and love. She is open to being persuaded by God rather than a boyfriend. Once a relationship with a guy enters the picture, things begin to change. Her thoughts become: "What can I do for him?" or "How can I make him notice me or love me more?" She is no longer focused on God but on the guy of her dreams. Once you have been in a dating relationship, you would probably agree with me that the relationship has the ability to completely take over everything in your life. If you are not careful when the new guy enters the picture, your quiet time with God will begin to suffer. When QT suffers, you miss out on what the Lord wants to tell you about your life.

On the other hand, a woman that is married is busy trying to make her husband happy. Think about your mom or another married woman that is in your life. Most of them probably spend their day doing something for him or the family (cleaning, working to help support the family, running errands, and more). Now don't get me wrong; there is a lot of honor in being in a godly marriage and being a wife. It should be the goal of our lives if you desire to be married later. However, during the teen years, your focus should be on growing closer with God so that when you are married, you will have a solid foundation of self-worth, love, respect, and happiness needed to have a godly marriage. You can't offer the best of yourself if you don't have a solid relationship with God. The time to develop that relationship is now.

God wants you to learn who you are and what makes you tick *before* you go into a dating relationship. When you date someone, you spend energy and time finding out what makes another person who they are, which causes you to miss out on your own journey. This is why you should accomplish your self-discovery first and then begin the dating process. Dating is a personal choice, but I hope you will wait until God leads you to date. I spent my entire teen years dating. I was not "happy" unless I was in a relationship. There was no balance in my life. Dating was my identity. If the boyfriend was happy, I was happy. If he was mad at someone, I was mad at them too.

Dating Up Close

Before we go on, let's take a little trip into history together. In the 1800s, *courting* was the popular expression of love. A young man was allowed only to spend supervised time with the young woman of his dreams by walking together, riding together (on separate horses, not in cars), and visiting "in the parlor." In the early 1900s, things began to loosen slightly. Young ladies began going to dances with young men (probably meeting them there). In the 1920s, with the invention of the automobile, dating found its way into society.

Dating was seen as the primary way of finding out if the guy you liked was marriage material. The way he treated you on a date was of utmost importance. Romance was an innocent form of expressing love. Most guys were considerate of girls, and girls loved all the new attention they received. The automobile began an entire new form of spending time together before marriage. Young men and women began going places together alone. Being alone together was heavily frowned upon before these times. Dating has escalated over the past 100-plus years to what you see now; it has not always been what you now know it as.

Today's culture defines dating as one-night stands, control and manipulation, and the full benefits of being married without the commitment. Today, dating is not even used for what it was originally created: finding your husband or wife for life. Believe it or not, dating is meant to be a way of deciding if someone is potentially suitable as a future spouse. It is not meant to be a way to experiment sexually, to compromise your moral beliefs, or to "try on" other lifestyles. Dating is simply meant to find out more about the person you are considering as an applicant for marriage—kind of like going on a job interview. You should aim to find a guy that you can talk with for hours and hours. As you grow older, communication will be what sustains you and your relationship.

Another common practice in the past and among royalty is arranged marriages. I often teased my daughters when they were younger that they should be glad they do not live in a culture that arranges marriages. I would have loved to pick their future husbands! Arranged marriages controlled the bloodline or royal heritage within the family. The king and queen would select another royal family to betroth their son or daughter in an effort to secure their place in line for the throne. The missing link there was love. I am sure you can grow to love another, but love just doesn't happen due to a mere arrangement.

I want to challenge your faith here for a second. Really think about these questions!

Ask It: If God created you in His image, then you must be mighty important to Him, right? Would God not take the time to create another human to compliment you specifi-cally? Would God just stop and say, "Hey, girl! Good luck finding a husband out there. Make me proud, would ya?"

She brings him good, not harm, all the days of her life.

Proverbs 31:12 (NLT)

Proverbs 31 says every day we live should be lived out to honor your future husband, even before you meet him. If you go on a date, remember this verse. Your life doesn't begin the day you get married. Your life includes every day from the day you were born, not just the day you say "I do." If you are thinking about holding your date's hand or kissing him, first ask yourself, "Would this honor my future husband?" Remember, your future husband is out there, and he could be dating other girls too at this moment. How would you want your future husband to handle his date? If you want him to be pure, then you should be pure too. Regardless if you have or have not met him yet, whatever you would expect of him, you should expect nothing less of yourself. Here are some dating dos and don'ts:

- Say *no* to the blanket. Always!
- Your parents are cooler than you think. It's okay to hang out with them too.
- House dates are never cool. Group dates are.
- If Dad doesn't like him, then walk away… quickly.
- Always leave room for the Holy Ghost.
- (Create your own idea and add it to the list.)

A word of warning: If you feel that you can or need to change a guy, you are off to destruction. Seek a guy that doesn't need to be repaired, tuned up, or downright over-hauled. Do not start your dating life in the shop. A healthy friendship is the best way to start any relationship. I once heard someone say, "Best friends make best marriages." I think there is truth to the saying. Don't skip the friendship to rush into relationship. One verse in the Bible that fits dating is found in 1 Corinthians 15:33, which says, *"Don't be fooled by those who say such things, for 'bad company corrupts good character.'"* Bad company is never a good thing, regardless of how you try to justify it.

My suggestion is to wait for Mr. Right. God has secretly crafted him just for you. God has amazing plans for your life. Some of those plans may include your future husband, while some plans may not. Please keep it in perspective. We should look forward to Jesus-style dating. Be strong enough to admit it if you are not ready to date yet. Dating, in the right context and at the right time, is a beautiful thing. It is a time that you learn more about the likes and dislikes of your potential future spouse, and they learn more about you too. It should be one of the most wonderful times of your life.

Check It:

- Take time to write a letter to God telling Him about your concerns for dating. Ask Him to show you what *His* intentions are for your dating life. Remember, this would be God's intentions, not necessarily your own.

- Go over the questions found in this chapter. Spend some time answering them in your journal.

Store It:

Pick your favorite version for this *Store It:*

> Wait patiently for the Lord. Be brave and courageous. Yes, wait patiently for the Lord.
>
> Psalm 27:14 (NLT)

> Stay with God! Take heart. Don't quit. I'll say it again: Stay with God!
>
> Psalm 27:14 (MSG)

The future belongs to those who believe in the beauty of their dreams.

—Eleanor Roosevelt

MR. RIGHT

There, my diary sat calling my name. I liked to scribble my thoughts and random ideas down on occasion. Today was one of those occasions. I opened to a blank page and began to write:

Dear Diary,

I want to meet THE perfect guy for me. One who will love me for who I am, like the same stuff I like, and never lie to me. Is there really such a guy out there? If so, where is he? Please tell me there is a guy for me out there somewhere. Sometimes I wonder.

Love,
me

I closed the book, locked the tiny lock, and hid the key. I put the book on the shelf and shut my eyes. Would I ever meet Mr. Right?

When you read the title of this chapter, I imagine you immediately pictured in your mind this perfect guy that likely looks like some *hottie* from Hollywood. The comical part is not one person envisions the same image. Since each of us is created differently with unique desires and characteristics, we each desire something different, and that's a good thing. Thankfully, there is an entire ocean of guys with different characteristics to choose from to compliment you in marriage if this is in God's future for you.

Characteristics of a Godly Husband

The characteristics of a godly husband are truly desirable. The Bible tells us in Psalm 37:4 (NLT) to *"Take delight in the Lord, and He will give you your heart's desires."* When we delight ourselves in God, we begin to seek the characteristics in others that He desires for us, and the rest just falls into place. These captivating characteristics are life giving and compliment our own character. Kind of like salt and pepper. Each one is good separately, but together, salt and pepper are a winning combo. They do not complete one another since they are distinctly different; however, when united, they enhance the flavor of the other.

The characteristics of a godly husband are not only desirable, but they are nonnegotiable. Below, I've listed a few of the nonnegotiable qualities or characteristics you should look for in your Mr. Right. All of these qualities should not be negotiated in the least. Don't get me wrong; there are negotiable characteristics of your Mr. Right. For example, what color his hair and eyes are, if he's short or tall, or if he's funny, smart, or athletic. Those things don't really matter and are based on your personal preference. Just make sure what you desire is what God desires for you. Ask God what kind of guy He wants you to be with. After all, God knows what you desire; He created you. Don't get hung up on Mr. Right's looks, though. Remember from "Beautiful from the Inside Out" that "real beauty is in the eye of the beholder." Don't limit a guy because of his height, weight, or hair/eye color combo.God will give you the desires of your heart. Please trust God on this one. If God created you inside and out, and God wrote all of the days of your life in His book before you were born (check out Psalm 139 about this), then don't you think that God is capable of having the perfect guy already planned for you? Remember, you were created to be pursued, not to be the pursuer. Give God credit in this area (and a chance).

Here is what I feel could be the top seven characteristics of a godly *Mr. Right*:

Spirit-Filled

> Don't team up with those who are unbelievers. How can righteousness be a partner with wickedness? How can light live with darkness? What harmony can there be between Christ and the devil? How can a believer be a partner with an unbeliever?"
>
> 2 Corinthians 6:14–15 (NLT)

The first thing you should seek in a guy is that he is in relationship with God and lives by the strength of the Holy Spirit. *No exceptions!* This means he should have a regular prayer life, seek quiet time with God, and hear from Him regularly. He needs to be filled with the Holy Spirit, which means that he has accepted Christ as his Savior and has asked the Holy Spirit to live inside him. You will know if he has really done this by his fruit (his actions, character, and words).

He should be plugged into the Word and not ashamed to admit any of it, and he should be sold out to Jesus. If he's not in love with God, then you better run like a wild woman being chased by bees! This should be priority. If his story is "I'm too busy to make it to church because of practice or my job," then girls, you need to reconsider. Don't be deceived by a guy that simply "believes" in God. Anyone can believe there is a God; even the devil acknowledges God is real. The real question is does he *know* Jesus and have a relationship with Him? You should seek a godly man who will lead you toward God and not away from Him. Imagine what kind of a husband and/or father he will be in the future.

Considerate

> Don't be selfish; don't try to impress others. Be humble, thinking of others as better than yourselves.
>
> Philippians 2:3 (NLT)

Your Mr. Right should be respectful. When he comes to the door, he should greet your parents with honor, and he should highly regard your parents' wishes and advice. Mr. Right should believe in the lost art of chivalry—you know, like opening the door for you … need I go on? He should be concerned with your happiness, as well as his own, and treat you like a lady. In order to make sure he has this quality, pay attention to the way he treats girls in everyday life situations (at school, at work, at church) and especially watch how he treats his mom! The way he treats his mom will speak a lot on how considerate he will be once the newness wears off of your relationship.

Generous

> ...For God loves a person who gives cheerfully.
>
> 2 Corinthians 9:7 (NLT)

Generosity must be a definite! A guy who loves God is going to want to give like God. He is not going to be unsympathetic with others or stingy toward those in need. Instead, your Mr. Right should care for people and show love toward others. He should be helpful to his friends when they are in need, and he volunteers in his church and shouldn't be afraid of serving. Pay attention to how he handles his money. What does he buy? Do those things always revolve around him, or does he use his time and funds to serve other people as well? His spending patterns will speak volumes about his level of generosity. Always remember that a person's heart is attached to their debit card. You usually put your money where your priorities are. Your Mr. Right's actions should always speak louder than his words.

Confident

> I want you woven into a tapestry of love, in touch with everything there is to know of God. Then you will have minds confident and at rest, focused on Christ, God's great mystery.
>
> Colossians 2:2 (MSG)

Confidence is so attractive. Your Mr. Right should be secure in who he is as a person. Confidence allows your guy to know when to say no and the courage to do so. It keeps balance in his life. A confident guy is unafraid of what others think about him and does not have to prove himself to his friends. He will not have to act differently based on who is around at the moment. You will know he is secure by the way he makes decisions. If he is secure with himself, he will not worry about what others think of him while seeking to please God. A godly guy knows how to have fun and keep it clean. He doesn't need to engage in inappropriate activities to discover who he is because he already knows who he is.

Arrogance or conceit is not confidence. When guys are self-centered or overly prideful, it is usually a sign that they are insecure with themselves. Confidence is belief in yourself and your abilities in a positive way. It will gain your trust where arrogance will not.

Encouraging

> Don't use foul or abusive language. Let everything you say be good and helpful, so that your words will be an encouragement to those who hear them.
>
> Ephesians 4:29 (NLT)

Mr. Right should use words that are uplifting. He should try to speak life-building words to the girl he loves, as well as everyone else. He should compliment his girl for who God created her to be. He should say things that are appropriate for any audience. He shouldn't tear you (or others) down with his words, nor should he be constantly critical or negative. He will always make you feel good about who you are. He should never leave you feeling ashamed, torn down, or belittled.

Gentle

> Always be humble and gentle. Be patient with each other, making allowance for each other's faults because of your love.
>
> Ephesians 4:2 (NLT)

When your guy is gentle, he will not be controlling or abusive. He shouldn't try to manipulate situations to get his way either. He should always allow you the freedom to be yourself. The guy you fall for shouldn't mind that you do things regularly with your girl friends. Gentle guys are not jealous but instead trust you at all times. Your Mr. Right shouldn't feel that he owns you and your every moment belongs to him. Girls, be aware of the fine line of wanting to spend time with you and wanting all of your time. I encourage you to look for a guy who doesn't want to control or manipulate all of your choices.

Here's a little tip: If you need his approval for things, you need to run as fast as you can from him! If a guy is ever abusive toward you (verbally, physically, emotionally, or sexually), I want you to break it off with him immediately. If you don't feel safe to do so, then you need to speak with an adult you trust and, if necessary, the authorities to make a plan to get out of that relationship.

The guy you are with should like you just the way you are and handle you with extreme care. He should have no need or desire to change you. Have the mindset that it is a privilege for him to even have the opportunity to spend time with you.

Pure

> Everything is pure to those whose hearts are pure. But nothing is pure to those who are corrupt and unbelieving, because their minds and consciences are corrupted.
>
> Titus 1:15 (NLT)

Your guy should desire to live God's version of purity rather than the world's counterfeit version. He shouldn't want to pollute himself with offensive music or impure shows or movies. He shouldn't use foul language or speak about dirty things. He should live to please Jesus in all areas of his life. Remember, his actions always speak louder than his words.

Your Mr. Right should never pressure you or any of his dates into anything he would not desire for his wife before their wedding. If your guy is pure, he will respect his own body, as well as his date's body, and will regard his body as a temple of the Holy Spirit that's living within him. He should never force his sexual opinion upon others and should guard his virginity and purity for his future wife.

Praying For Your Future Husband

Wow! Those are only a few of the godly traits you should seek. There are many more. Remember he is only human. He will not be called Mr. Perfect, only Mr. Right. The list above offers a great start for finding out if your Mr. Right has the right qualities, but how can you ensure that you will end up with someone like that? The answer begins not only seeking those qualities but with praying for your future husband. Seek God's heart for His desire for your future.

First Peter 3:12 says, *"The eyes of the Lord watch over those who do right, and his ears are open to their prayers."*

God is constantly listening to the prayers of His people. Our prayers are that important to God! When we speak to Him, He is ready and waiting to hear our requests. It doesn't mean that He will give you every single thing you ask for or want; praying for a million dollars to fall from the sky or a shiny new sports car for your birthday is likely not going to happen. However, when we seek pure lives and truly make our hearts' request, I believe He not only hears our prayers but takes note of our desires as well.

Just as it's hard to walk in your own shoes at times, your future husband may have hurdles of his own to leap over. Ask God to strengthen him every day in whatever he is facing. Seek God on his behalf every time you think about it. When you pray for your future husband, don't hold back. Remember, God is watching and listening. Pray big! You should request things like security in him, peace in his life, and strength in his walk with God. Ask for a lifestyle of purity to be important to your Mr. Right. Pray for blessings to be poured out on him. It certainly cannot hurt! Intercede for him in areas you want your husband to be strong in. If marriage is in God's future plans for you, He will certainly honor your requests.

Here are a couple of tips for praying for your future husband:

- Do not be afraid to ask God for what you want. Go boldly to Him, asking for the desires of your heart. Tell God what it is you would like in your future husband.

- Ask more than once; keep praying every day for your future man. Make a list of the qualities you want or journal about them. Make it a long-term project and not just a one-time demand.

- Don't spend your entire prayer time talking. Spend time listening to God about what He desires for your future. Get to know His voice well.

I cannot stress enough how important prayer is. I know a young woman who would ask God day after day to send her a godly husband. Some days she felt as if her prayers were never going to be answered. On other days, she had complete confidence in God. After requesting and seeking God for what seemed like decades, God finally crossed her path with her dream guy. Her advice to you would be to pray, pray, pray for your future husband! It really does make a difference.

Sitting at God's feet transforms the inside of us and changes our view. I know you've heard the phrase "prayer changes things." I really believe this. Prayer opens your eyes to see the pollution this world attempts to inject into our hearts. You begin to seek after the pure things that are important to God. A wise woman I know and admire repeatedly says, "When you are on your knees, there's only one direction to look...*up!*" When you seek God and delight yourself with Him, He truly gives you the wishes of your heart because your desires become what He desires. Take some time to see things from God's perspective. Take a stroll through God's Word and study the numerous stories of people that camped out at God's feet.

Remember to ask, ask again, and listen! *"Pray all the time"* (1 Thessalonians 5:17 MSG). As you pray for your future husband, may God grant you the desires of your heart and fill you with abundant love—more than you can contain, hope for, or even imagine!

Check It:

- Pray and ask God what He desires for your *Mr. Right*, and then make a list of the qualities you'd like to find in him. They can be negotiable or non-negotiable qualities. Be as picky as you'd like, just make sure you don't put God in a box by centering all of the qualities on looks.

- What do you expect from Mr. Right? Are you living by the same standards?

Store It:

Take delight in the Lord, and he will give you your heart's desires.

Psalm 37:4 (NLT)

The way to preserve the peace of the church is to preserve its purity.

—Matthew Henry

GUARDING FROM THE FALL

As I walked down the aisle on my Dad's arm, my mind was flooded with so many thoughts. I began thinking of our breakfast together earlier in the day.

Dad insisted we go to breakfast together one last time as a family before the wedding. My dad was not a man of many words in my youth, but he had some things to express this particular morning. He looked across the table and said, "You don't have to do this. A baby is no reason to get married. If you have the slightest doubt, we can cancel everything. No questions."

Wow! No pressure, Dad?! As I looked across the table, full of fear but certain about one thing, I wondered, How did I get here? *This was like a one big crazy dream I couldn't wake up from. At that moment, I knew I didn't want any of my friends to walk this route, or at least, the ones I had left.*

Pregnant, 18, and about to be married, I carried a lot of guilt and shame. The regret of poor and uninformed decisions was heavy. The path I was walking wasn't one

I had ever dreamed or desired for my future—at least not in this order. The consequences of my decisions were huge and lifelong. Purity was my heart's desire, but somehow I stepped off of that route along the way. If I learned anything, I knew I didn't want to see others walk the same path of hurt and confusion. I had learned my lesson the hard way.

So now that you've reached the last chapter of the book, hopefully you learned a lot along the way about loving yourself and the meaning of purity. We've talked about things like:

- Godly purity in an ungodly world
- The Sparkle
- Making good decisions
- Getting connected in your local church
- Dating and some characteristics of Mr. Right

Even with all this great information, you still need to know a few final elements in order to avoid falling into the trap of impurity. Relax! This may be one of the easier chapters we've walked through together on this journey, but don't let it fool you. It's just like the paint job on your car. If the paint doesn't have a clear coat or seal on it, the paint will easily crack and fade, leaving your sparkling beauty dull and lifeless. Purity is much like the paint on the car—you need to seal it in order to protect it.

You might ask, "How can I do that?" Actually, the answer is easy. God's Word tells us many ways of guarding from the fall. When you committed your life to God, He made you brand spanking new. He desires for you to be a shining billboard to others of His great love, to sparkle.

One way to guard from the fall is to *avoid* it. Like we discussed in "The Sparkle," God says, "Run from sexual sin" (1 Corinthians 6:18 (NLT)). He doesn't want you to play with fire. It may sparkle, but it burns, leaving you with a scar. In 2 Timothy 2:22 (NLT), we also find instruction to *"Run from anything that stimulates youthful lust. Instead, pursue righteous living, faithfulness, love, and peace. Enjoy the companionship of those who call on the Lord with pure hearts."* If we pursue righteous living (integrity, honor, innocence, holiness), faith (belief, hope, truth), love (devotion, respect, worship), and peace (brotherhood, friendship, unity) with other committed followers of Jesus, we develop accountability. Accountability is key!

Another biggie is found in 1 Thessalonians 4:3–4 (NLT), which says, *"God's will is for you to be holy, so stay away from all sexual sin. Then each of you will control his own body and live in holiness and honor."* Control is the key. If you keep in mind at all times that it is your priority to do your best to control your body in a way that is holy and honorable, you have a better chance of avoiding getting into a passionate situation. Remember, self-control is one of the Fruit of the Spirit, and as you pursue purity, you will develop this. If you need a refresher, review "What God's Word Says about Purity."

Two Steps to Clarity

A lasting lifestyle of purity can be wrapped up in two final steps: establishing accountability and setting a standard.

Step 1: Establish Accountability

Accountability is *vital* to remaining pure. Seek out others sharing your desire to be pure. When you are weak, they can help you focus. Likewise, when they feel tempted, you can help them stay on track. It can be a win-win situation.

If you've been involved in an impure relationship, it's almost impossible to stay pure in the old circumstances. Once you've made a commitment to be pure, you should seek God's direction regarding your relationships/friendships, and then *take* God's advice.

My friend's mom always said, "You are who you hang with." It's probably one of the biggest truths I've ever heard. We tried to prove her wrong but never could. The truth is there is strength in numbers. Be selective of the people you hang out with. Another mom said, "You are the average of those you hang around." Think about that one. If you assigned a number on the "good" to "bad" scale for each of your friends, what's your average? First Corinthians 15:33 (NLT) reminds us of an important rule of thumb: *"Don't be fooled by those who say such things, for 'bad company corrupts good character.'"* The chick you pick to stand with you should have the same morals and beliefs stated in God's Word. Make sure they are not pulling you away from your decision to remain pure but encouraging and supporting you to follow your standard.

Step 2: Set a Standard

This final step is equally as important as step one. Establish a standard for yourself, put it in writing, and sign it! So what are standards? Standards are morals or principles that you decide are acceptable, boundaries in life that you will live by. They are like armor, so to speak. When it's properly fitted and worn, armor protects you and helps prevent injury. Don't set your standards so high that you will fail, and don't think that you are ruined if you do fail. My dad gave me some great advice recently, and I will pass it along to you: "We all make mistakes. It's not how you fall down that counts, but it's how you get back up!" If you have made bad decisions in the past, do not let them hold you back. Once you confess those sins to God, they are thrown into the sea of forgetfulness (Micah 7:19 (NLT)). God forgets our sin because Jesus steps in to cover the sin with His blood. God no longer sees that sin, but sees Jesus's blood instead. He does not love you less when you sin. He loved you the same yesterday as He does today and will love you tomorrow!

> Once again you will have compassion on us. You will trample our sins under your feet and throw them into the depths of the ocean!
>
> Micah 7:19 (NLT)

Your standard might include stuff like what values you hold as important, what your boundaries will be when you enter into a dating relationship, what age you intend to be before you go on dates, and so on. What will it cost to be pure? Every good thing in life costs something, and the really desirable things can cost a lot. You may have to consider giving up your boyfriend or a best friend who tempts you to be impure. Perhaps you will have to stop going places that cause you to be impure or even give up certain TV shows, movies, and/or music that make you think impure thoughts. Whatever the cost, it will be worth it, I assure you.

Once you establish your standard, take time to read it at least once a week and definitely before you go out with friends or on a date. Share it with your parents and the person you are accountable to from step one. Hang it in your room. Keep it right were you can find it immediate.

Final Thoughts

Following the guidelines and suggestions in this book are a great way to guard your life. It is merely a diving board into a lifestyle of purity. Always remember that purity is a choice. It is a principle that has lots of reward. As I've urged you in the previous pages, please pray about what you've read and seek the advice of godly women in your life. Purity is not a decision you should take lightly.

Keep storing those verses because God's Word is the owner's manual for our lives. It will certainly help you in the upcoming battles you will face. I'd also like to encourage you to keep journaling your thoughts. Some of the greatest role models journal their views and daily events of their lives. Just like in the *Check It* sections, you can do multiple things. You can write letters to Jesus about how you feel, create poems about His love in your life, and maybe even write songs. When you believe God is speaking to you, write that down especially. It's great to have all of these entries in your journal to remind yourself of God's love on your not-so-great days.

Girls, I love you, and I believe in you. Take a stand in your school and community for purity and change your world. It's truly been a great honor and blessing to share this adventure with you. It's up to you to continue your journey now. May you sparkle like diamonds!

Check It:

- Complete your standard and get accountable to someone! Ask God to help you with the steps. Share this with your mentor, if you have one, or your parents.

- Once you've completed the above, spend some time journaling one thought that you learned from each chapter. How has it affected your walk with Jesus and your view of purity?

Store It:

Don't let anyone think less of you because you are young. Be an example to all believers in what you say, in the way you live, in your love, your faith, and your purity.

1 Timothy 4:12 (NLT)

Our deepest fear is not that we are inadequate. Our deepest fear is that we are powerful beyond measure. It is our light, not our darkness that most frightens us. We ask ourselves, "Who am I to be brilliant, gorgeous, talented, fabulous?" Actually, who are you not to be? You are a child of God.

—Marianne Williamson

My Prayer

Father God, it's been an unbelievable trip throughout the pages of Your heart. Some of the steps were difficult while others brought delight. Our hearts and minds have been molded by Your Word, leaving a trail of Your fingerprints farther than we can see or imagine. Jesus, I pray for each person that reads these pages to be transformed by Your Word. May she always desire to hide Your Word in her heart as a shield against sin. Open her eyes to see the unquenchable love You have for her. Show her just how valuable she truly is in Your eyes. May she hold on to the real beauty You created within her and see that she is fearfully and wonderfully made. Jesus, as she seeks You, fill every empty spot in her heart until it overflows like a raging flood into the lives around her. Strengthen her in her weak areas and equip her to stand up and change her world. May she be a mirror of Your love as she pursues your freedom! I ask You to seal her with Your Holy Spirit. Show up in her life in a way that only You can and bless her beyond her wildest dreams! May she be proud to be a princess of the Most High King Jesus and represent You and Your kingdom well! Thank You from the bottom of my heart for allowing me to be a part of this amazing adventure. May every ounce of praise and glory honor You, my sweet Savior Jesus! I pray this in Your precious name, Jesus! Amen.

For additional information, please go
to www.conniefirmin.com.

If this book has helped you, send us your
story. We'd love to hear about it. E-mail
us at conniefirmin@gmail.com.

ENDNOTES

1. http://dictionary.reference.com/browse/purity

   American Psychological Association (APA): purity. (n.d.). *Dictionary.com Unabridged*. Retrieved September 08, 2010, from Dictionary.com website: **http://dictionary.reference.com/browse/purity**

   Chicago Manual Style (CMS): purity. Dictionary. com. *Dictionary.com Unabridged*. Random House, Inc. **http://dictionary.reference.com/browse/purity** (accessed: September 08, 2010).

   Modern Language Association (MLA): "purity." *Dictionary.com Unabridged*. Random House, Inc. 08 Sep. 2010. <Dictionary.com **http://dictionary.reference. com/browse/purity**>.

   Institute of Electrical and Electronics Engineers (IEEE): Dictionary.com, "purity," in *Dictionary.com Unabridged*. Source location: Random House, Inc. **http://dictionary.reference.com/browse/purity**.

Available: **http://dictionary.reference.com**. Accessed: September 08, 2010.

BibTeX Bibliography Style (BibTeX): @article {Dictionary.com2010, title = {Dictionary.com Unabridged}, month = {Sep}, day = {08}, year = {2010}, url = {**http://dictionary.reference.com/browse/purity**},}

2. http://www.cdc.gov/Features/dsTeenPregnancy/ #source Hamilton BE, Martin JA, Ventura SJ. Births: Preliminary data for 2007. National vital statistics reports; vol 57 no 12. Hyattsville, MD: National Center for Health Statistics. 2009.